GW00418497

This edition copyright © 2001 Lion Publishing
Illustrations copyright © 2001 Anita Burman

Published by
**Lion Publishing plc**
Sandy Lane West, Oxford, England
www.lion-publishing.co.uk
ISBN 0 7459 4737 9

This edition 2001
1 3 5 7 9 10 8 6 4 2 0

All rights reserved

**Music acknowledgments**

℗ 2000 Classic Fox Records.
Recording under licence from Classic Fox Records,
1, Collington Avenue, Bexhill, East Sussex, TN39 3PX, England.

**Text acknowledgments**

12: from *The Alternative Service Book 1980*, copyright © 1980
The Central Board of Finance of the Church of England and
reproduced by permission.

14, 15, 22, 28: Song of Songs 8:6–7, Song of Songs 2:10–13,
Philippians 2:1–11, I Corinthians 13:1–8, 13, from the *Holy Bible,
New International Version*, copyright © 1973, 1978, 1984 by
International Bible Society. Used by permission.

16: Ecclesiastes 4:9–10, from the Good News Bible published by
The Bible Societies/HarperCollins Publishers Ltd, UK © American
Bible Society 1966, 1971, 1976, 1992, used with permission.

A catalogue record for this book is available
from the British Library

Typeset in 11.5/22 Apple Chancery
Printed and bound in Singapore

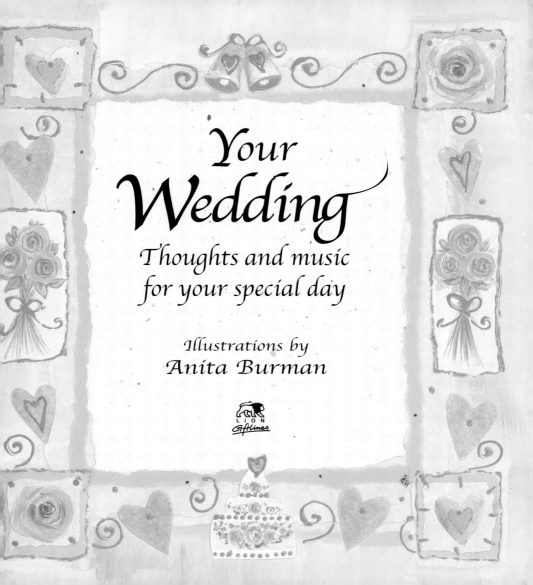

# Your Wedding

## Thoughts and music for your special day

Illustrations by
**Anita Burman**

LION
Giftlines

# Contents

# Introduction

*Love is like the
blood pulsing through
the veins of marriage.
It makes it alive.*

Walter Trobisch

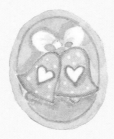

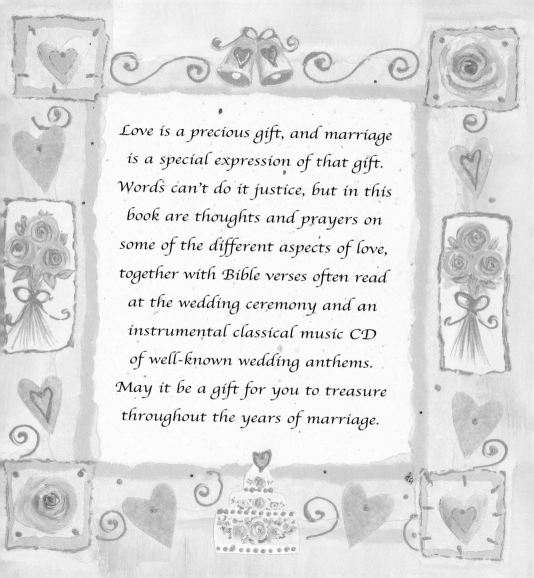

Love is a precious gift, and marriage
is a special expression of that gift.
Words can't do it justice, but in this
book are thoughts and prayers on
some of the different aspects of love,
together with Bible verses often read
at the wedding ceremony and an
instrumental classical music CD
of well-known wedding anthems.
May it be a gift for you to treasure
throughout the years of marriage.

# Love

Love alone is capable of uniting
living beings in such a way as
to complete and fulfil them, for it
alone takes them and joins them
by what is deepest in themselves.

*Pierre Teilhard de Chardin*

Love, all alike,
no season knows, nor clime,
Nor hours, days, months,
which are the rags of time.

*John Donne*

Love is honey;
how sweet it is to the soul.

*Author unknown*

To love is to receive a glimpse of heaven.

*Karen Sunde*

In love the paradox occurs that
two beings become one and yet remain two.

*Erich Fromm*

# Comfort

Love is an act of endless forgiveness,
a tender look which becomes a habit.

*Peter Ustinov*

Marriage is given, that husband and wife
may comfort and help each other, living faithfully
together in need and in plenty, in sorrow and in joy.

*The Alternative Service Book*

Love consists in this, that two solitudes
protect and touch and greet each other.

*Rainer Maria Rilke*

Grant that I
may not so much
seek to be consoled,
as to console;
to be understood,
as to understand;
to be loved, as to love.

St Francis of Assisi

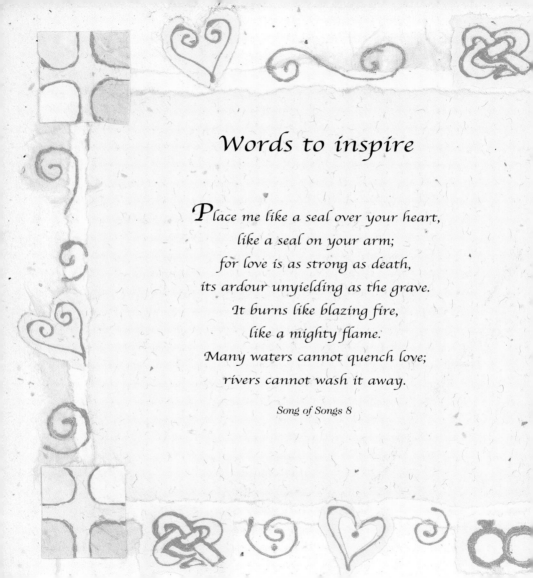

# Words to inspire

$P$lace me like a seal over your heart,
like a seal on your arm;
for love is as strong as death,
its ardour unyielding as the grave.
It burns like blazing fire,
like a mighty flame.
Many waters cannot quench love;
rivers cannot wash it away.

*Song of Songs 8*

My lover spoke and said to me,
'Arise, my darling,
my beautiful one, and come with me.
See! The winter is past;
the rains are over and gone.
Flowers appear on the earth;
the season of singing has come,
the cooing of doves is heard in our land.
The fig tree forms its early fruit;
the blossoming vines spread their fragrance.
Arise, come, my darling;
my beautiful one, come with me.'

*Song of Songs 2*

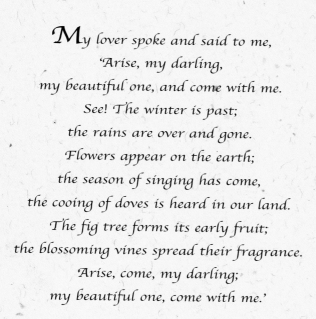

# Encouragement

Two are better off than
one, because together they
can work more effectively.
If one of them falls down,
the other can help him up.

*The Bible*

Love is a fragile thing.
It must be maintained and
protected if it is to survive.

*James Dobson*

If I could reach up and hold a
star for every time you've made
me smile, the entire evening sky
would be in the palm of my hand.

*Author unknown*

Love's pure silver flame gives each
innermost spirit invisible warmth.

*Haiku verse*

# Sharing

Marriage... two people making a
present of their whole lives to each other.

*Robert Runcie*

My bounty is as boundless as the sea,
My love as deep. The more I give to thee,
The more I have, for both are infinite.

*William Shakespeare*

Love is action, not thought.

*Paul Tournier*

'To become one flesh'
means that two persons share
everything they have, not only
their bodies, not only their
material possessions, but also
their thinking and their feeling,
their joy and their suffering,
their hopes and their fears, their
successes and their failures.

Walter Trobisch

# Commitment

The great ideals, of which
faithfulness is one, are great
realities, not vague hopes.
They need to grow as a harvest
with patient cultivation.

*Robert Runcie*

Love is not love that alters
where it alteration finds.

*William Shakespeare*

 Love is not the feeling
of a moment
but the conscious decision
of a way of life.

*Ulrich Schaffer*

I've fallen in love many times...
always with you.

*Author unknown*

The heart that has truly loved never forgets
But as truly loves on to the close.

*Thomas More*

# Words to inspire

**I**f you have any encouragement from being united with Christ, if any comfort from his love, if any fellowship with the Spirit, if any tenderness and compassion, then make my joy complete by being like-minded, having the same love, being one in spirit and purpose. Do nothing out of selfish ambition or vain conceit, but in humility consider others better than yourselves. Each of you should look not only to your own interests, but also to the interests of others.

Your attitude should be the same as that of Christ Jesus: who, being in very nature God, did not consider equality with God something to be grasped, but made himself nothing, taking the very nature of a servant, being made in human likeness. And being found in appearance as a man, he humbled himself and became obedient to death – even death on a cross! Therefore God exalted him to the highest place and gave him the name that is above every name, that at the name of Jesus every knee should bow, in heaven and on earth and under the earth, and every tongue confess that Jesus Christ is Lord, to the glory of God the Father.

*Philippians 2*

# Vulnerability

*Love makes your soul crawl*
*out from its hiding place.*

Zora Neale Hurston

*They do not love*
*that do not show their love.*

William Shakespeare

*To love means to forget oneself*
*entirely for the sake of another.*

Michel Quoist

To love at all is to be
vulnerable. Love anything,
and your heart will certainly
be wrung and possibly broken.
If you want to make sure of
keeping it intact, you must
give your heart to no one.

C.S. Lewis

# Growth

You learn to speak by speaking,
to study by studying, to run by
running, to work by working; and
just so you learn to love God and
man by loving. Begin as a mere
apprentice and the very power of
love will lead you on to become a
master of the art.

*St Francis de Sales*

Growth and change are
inescapable aspects of marriage.

*Jack Dominian*

Love must be renewed constantly.

*Ulrich Schaffer*

Love can go on growing until the last
moment of our lives and has no limitations.

*Jack Dominian*

We learn only from those we love.

*Johann Peter Eckermann*

# Words to inspire

*If* I speak in the tongues of men and of angels, but have not love, I am only a resounding gong or a clanging cymbal. If I have the gift of prophecy and can fathom all mysteries and all knowledge, and if I have a faith that can move mountains, but have not love, I am nothing. If I give all I possess to the poor and surrender my body to the flames, but have not love, I gain nothing.

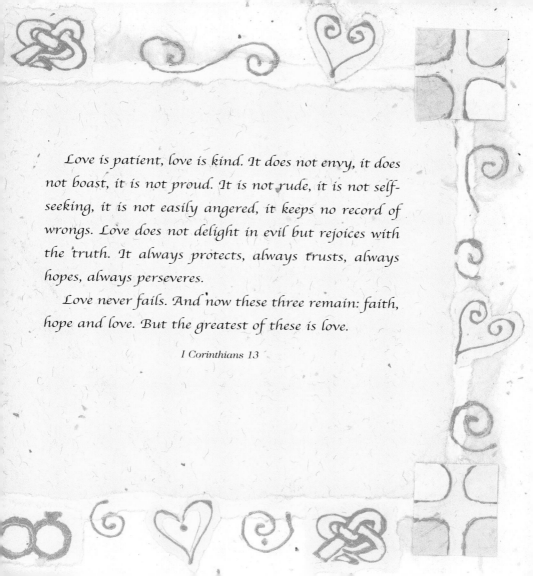

Love is patient, love is kind. It does not envy, it does not boast, it is not proud. It is not rude, it is not self-seeking, it is not easily angered, it keeps no record of wrongs. Love does not delight in evil but rejoices with the truth. It always protects, always trusts, always hopes, always perseveres.

Love never fails. And now these three remain: faith, hope and love. But the greatest of these is love.

*I Corinthians 13*

# Track titles

| | |
|---|---|
| Bridal March | Wagner |
| Jesu, Joy of Man's Desiring | J.S. Bach |
| Canon | Pachelbel |
| Trumpet Tune | Purcell |
| Water Music: Hornpipe | Handel |
| Wedding March | Mendelssohn |
| Prince of Denmark's March | Clarke |
| Arrival of the Queen of Sheba | Handel |
| Sheep May Safely Graze | J.S. Bach |
| Water Music: Air | Handel |